VICTORIA

'Vic' 'Tori' 'Ria'

by Diana Holt

illustrated by Josey Wawasniak

Grandma's Silver Series

 www.trafford.com

North America & international
toll-free: 1 888 232 4444 (USA & Canada)
fax: 812 355 4082

I would like to dedicate this book firstly to my children,

Don, Randy and Tim

They have been with me through thick and thin, and have shared all phases and challenges with me. Thank you boys, I love you!!

Secondly, to all of my

Grandchildren and Great Grandchildren

who have given me more joy, fun and memorable moments in my life than they know. They have taught me to love, laugh hard and often, and to find delight in the simplest of things.

 ## Thank You
to Josey Wawasniak
for the splendid illustrations.

A Special Thank You
to my many friends
for their endless continual encouragement.

Thank You to God
for being with me throughout my life, and never giving up on me.
My work would never have been completed without God's help.

Let's Pretend

VICTORIA

When I was a baby my Mommy and Daddy gave me a name.

My name is Victoria. I think Victoria is a pretty name, and everyone says that my name suits me. I like my name because I can pretend to be many people.

Daddy loves to call me by parts of my name.

Sometimes he calls me 'Vicki'.

'Vicki' is Daddy's girl. Some days he calls me 'Tori'.

I like it when my Daddy plays with me.

Other days Daddy calls me 'Ria'.

This is a name I never heard before.

When Daddy calls me 'Ria', I feel very different.

It makes me feel really special.

I feel like a Movie Star or someone very important, like a Princess or Prime Minister.

I think I like the name 'Ria' best, but sometimes I like to be 'Tori'. 'Tori' or 'Ria' could be a Nurse or School Teacher, or maybe a Scientist.

'Tori' is a little girl who likes to be mischievous,
and do silly things. 'Tori' loves cookies. 'Tori' likes
to do different things.

'Tori' likes to pretend to be a mommy, and so does 'Vicki'.

I have a brother who likes to call me 'Vic'.

'Vic' could be a boy's name. When my brother calls me 'Vic', I can pretend to be a boy and make believe I am his brother. We play cars and ride bikes. We pretend to be working on my brother's farm with his tractor and farm equipment.

It is fun to have a name like 'Victoria', because I can be a brother, a mischievous little girl, a sophisticated Movie Star, Daddy's little sweatheart or just be myself and be

VICTORIA.

I love to pretend.

Do you like to pretend?

Who or what would you like to be?

Printed in the United States
By Bookmasters